W9-ACU-869

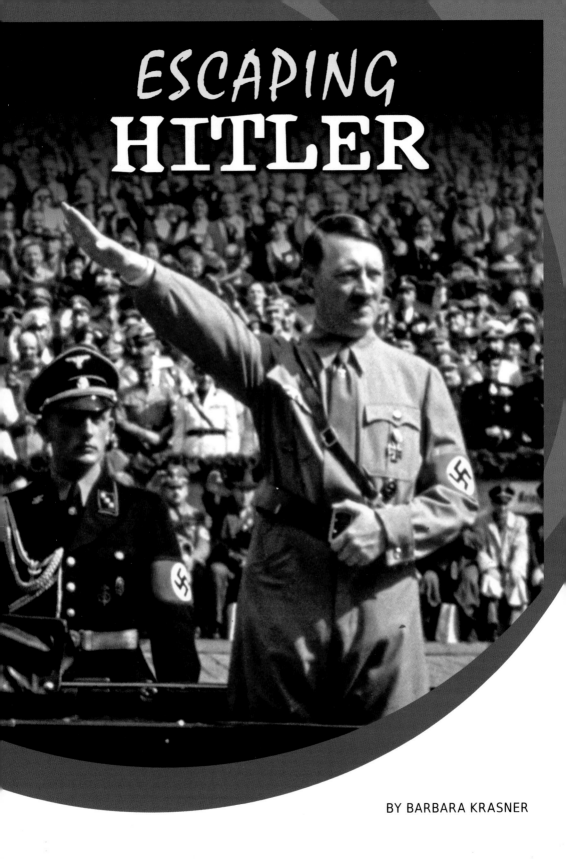

ESCAPING
HITLER

BY BARBARA KRASNER

Published by The Child's World®
1980 Lookout Drive • Mankato, MN 56003-1705
800-599-READ • www.childsworld.com

ISBN 9781503825277
LCCN 2017959691

Printed in the United States of America
PA02377

TABLE OF
CONTENTS

FAST FACTS

- Adolf Hitler and his National Socialist Party (Nazis) rose to power in Germany in 1933.

- In 1935, Hitler introduced laws to exclude Jewish people from German life. One of the laws said that Jewish people were no longer German citizens.

- Germany invaded and occupied Poland and other countries starting in September 1939. This action sparked World War II (1939–1945).

- The Nazis established 40,000 camps and prisons. They forced Jewish people, political prisoners, and many others into these camps and prisons.

- The Nazis gathered Jewish people and forced them into 1,100 ghettos, or closed-off sections of towns and cities. Many ghettos were established in Polish cities, including Warsaw, Lodz, and Krakow.

- The Nazis began emptying the ghettos in the spring of 1943. They herded millions of people onto trains headed for **death camps** in Poland. These death camps included Auschwitz, Treblinka, Chelmno, Belzec, and Sobibor.

The Nazis forced people to wear stars to identify ▶ themselves as Jewish.

- Six million Jewish people and hundreds of thousands of others died at the hands of the Nazis. This mass killing became known as the Holocaust.

- Approximately 500,000 Jewish people managed to escape Hitler.

Chapter 1

NINA KLEIN

The platform at the Prague train station was crowded with parents, children, and suitcases. Seventeen-year-old Nina Klein stood among them with her parents. Ever since the Nazis had invaded Prague in March 1939, the city had felt less and less like home to Jewish people such as Nina and her family. Her home country, Czechoslovakia, did not even exist anymore. Now she lived in the Protectorate of Bohemia and Moravia, under Nazi rule. German soldiers patrolled the station.

All Nina's parents had told her was that she was going to England. She had not thought much about it. She was used to traveling. Besides, her mother said she would only be away for two or three months at the most. Her mother placed a diamond ring into her hand. She told Nina to keep it under her tongue until she reached England. Nina should not let anyone see it. If captured by the Nazis, her mother told her, she could use the ring to buy her freedom.

◄ **A memorial in Poland commemorates Jewish children who escaped the Nazis during World War II.**

▲ In Nazi-occupied countries, posters honoring Hitler were placed in many public places.

Children of all ages, most of them Jewish, boarded the cars of the train. Nina hesitated. She did not have to board. She could stay with her parents, she told herself. But her parents persisted.

As the train pulled away from the platform, children pressed against the windows. The younger ones cried. Many waved. Nina did not want to wave. She wanted to get off. She kept her eyes on her parents. They held onto each other for support. She watched them as long as she could.

Nina settled in for the four-day journey. She did exactly as her mother had instructed. She held the ring under her tongue as the train chugged away from Prague and into Germany on the first day. At the border, Nazi soldiers boarded the train. They started yelling in German. They looked through the children's luggage.

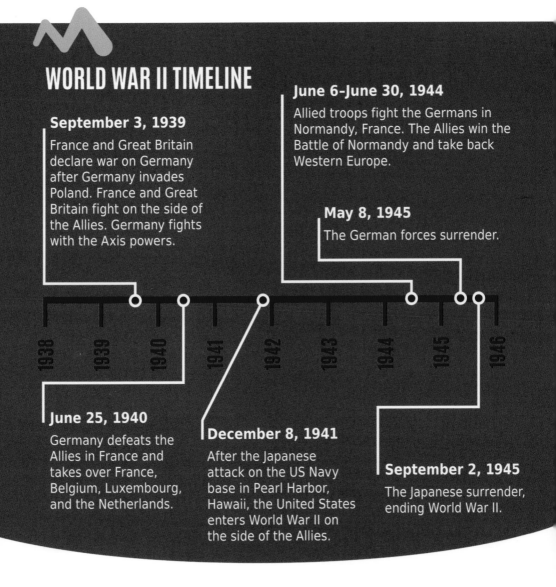

WORLD WAR II TIMELINE

September 3, 1939
France and Great Britain declare war on Germany after Germany invades Poland. France and Great Britain fight on the side of the Allies. Germany fights with the Axis powers.

June 6–June 30, 1944
Allied troops fight the Germans in Normandy, France. The Allies win the Battle of Normandy and take back Western Europe.

May 8, 1945
The German forces surrender.

1938 1939 1940 1941 1942 1943 1944 1945 1946

June 25, 1940
Germany defeats the Allies in France and takes over France, Belgium, Luxembourg, and the Netherlands.

December 8, 1941
After the Japanese attack on the US Navy base in Pearl Harbor, Hawaii, the United States enters World War II on the side of the Allies.

September 2, 1945
The Japanese surrender, ending World War II.

They sometimes dumped the contents of suitcases onto the ground. The children huddled against each other for safety.

Nina watched tall trees, wide rivers, and cathedrals rush by as the train passed through Germany on the second day. Every train station they entered scared her. Nazi soldiers and posters of Hitler were everywhere.

On the third day, the train arrived at its final destination. Nina stepped off in the Netherlands along the coast of the North Sea. Then she boarded a ferry to cross the English Channel. She had never seen such a large ship.

When they reached England, Nina and the other children took a train from the coast to London. The car doors opened. Adults standing behind a barrier on the platform called out names. Nina longed to see her parents' faces in the crowd. It was possible, she realized, to feel alone even in the midst of so many people.

A man called out Nina's name. He was Mr. Coates, a banker who had pledged to take care of her. He took her to his home in northwest England.

Nina did not know it at the time, but she was one of many children saved by British **diplomat** Sir Nicholas Winton. Winton had worked with the British Committee to Save Refugees from Czechoslovakia. He assembled lists of parents giving permission to save their children.

After the train left Prague, Nina Klein never saw her parents again. They were sent to Theresienstadt, a **concentration camp** approximately 38 miles (61 km) north of Prague. From there, they were sent to Auschwitz, where they later died.

In England, Nina met and married a fellow Czech. They returned to Prague after the war. She eventually moved to the United States.

WINTON AND THE KINDERTRANSPORT

Nicholas Winton gained inspiration for his rescue mission from the Kindertransport, a rescue mission led by the British government that saved 10,000 Jewish children between December 1938 and May 1940. Winton's rescue missions occurred in 1939. They involved transporting Jewish children from Czechoslovakia to London. Winton's first transports escaped by plane. Later transports escaped by train. By the end of World War II, Winton had saved 669 children.

Chapter 2

IRENA SENDLER

In the early morning hours of October 20, 1943, 33-year-old Irena Sendler woke up to someone pounding on the door of her house. Her mother, who had been sleeping next to her on the bed, cried out in alarm. The men on the other side of the door announced themselves as the Gestapo, the Nazi secret police. They demanded that Irena open the door.

Irena was prepared for this moment. Since the previous year, she had worked with a secret organization, Zegota, to smuggle Jewish children out of the Warsaw ghetto to safety. She gave them false, non-Jewish names. It was a dangerous operation. Helping Jewish people escape could mean death.

Eleven Gestapo agents filled the apartment and tore it apart. After a three-hour search, they dragged her outside and forced her into a prison van. She knew where they were going: the Nazi **interrogation** center on Szucha Avenue. Her heart thudded as the van bumped along the road.

◀ **Irena Sendler risked her life to help Jewish children escape Nazi-occupied Poland.**

When they arrived at the Nazi interrogation center, a tall Gestapo agent questioned Irena again and again in Polish. He wanted her to name the leaders of Zegota. The Gestapo broke her legs and feet. Still, she would not give names. She would not give in to fear or threats.

The next day, Irena was among the bruised and beaten taken by truck to the dreaded Pawiak Prison. She watched as the tall, gray walls of the prison came into view. She knew few prisoners ever survived in Pawiak.

During Irena's second day in prison, a member of the Polish **resistance** within the prison called out Irena's name. She told Irena to go to the prison dentist. Irena had no idea she had friends within the prison. But Irena soon realized that she recognized the dentist. She had known the dentist from before the war.

The dentist slipped Irena a note from Zegota's leaders. It said they were doing everything they could to get Irena out. Irena managed to write back that the lists she had kept of the real names, fake names, and whereabouts of the smuggled children were safe. She had hidden jars of these lists under an apple tree in a neighbor's yard.

Hermann Göring formed the Nazi secret police, the Gestapo, ▶ in 1933.

Irena did not allow herself to dream of freedom. She just wanted the torture to end. It was almost a relief when the Nazis sentenced her to death. One day in January 1944, she was brought to a dark waiting room with about 20 other women. The women's cries filled the air. One by one, women were called by name to face the firing squad.

Irena's name was called. She stumbled in the darkness. She heard only a clock ticking. She thought of her mother.

A guard motioned Irena into another room, where a Gestapo agent waited. She expected to face more interrogation. But the agent led her outdoors. He guided her across the street. Zegota's leaders had bribed officials at the prison to free Irena.

Stunned, Irena didn't know where to go. She was badly injured and could barely walk. She returned home. But Zegota's leaders convinced her to leave to ensure her mother's safety.

Irena assumed a new identity. Just like the children she had saved, she had to go into hiding. Throughout the rest of the war, she took refuge in many places, including the Warsaw Zoo. By the end of the war, Irena and other members of Zegota had helped more than 2,500 children escape Hitler.

◀ **The Museum of Pawiak Prison in Warsaw, Poland, shows what the prison looked like during World War II.**

Chapter 3

JACK AND ROCHELLE

Twenty-eight-year-old Jack Sutin knew Rochelle Schleiff would come to his underground **bunker** in the Naliboki Forest in Belarus. It came to him in a dream in August 1942. Rochelle was the young woman he had met briefly at a school dance in 1939 in Stolpce, her hometown in Poland. He wanted to date her, but she had refused. For all he knew, she died when the Nazis emptied out the Stolpce ghetto and sent the Jewish people to their deaths. Still, he prepared for her arrival, making room for her in the cramped bunker.

The Nazis had invaded Mir, Jack's hometown in Belarus, in 1941. Jack thought his mother would be safe. Although she was Jewish, she was a dentist, and the Nazis needed her services. But Jack and his father needed to hide so they wouldn't be forced into a ghetto. Jack found a farmhouse outside Mir where he could hide. His father found a place in the attic of a Christian family's house.

◄ **Jack Sutin poses in 2009 with a book about his and his wife's experiences during World War II.**

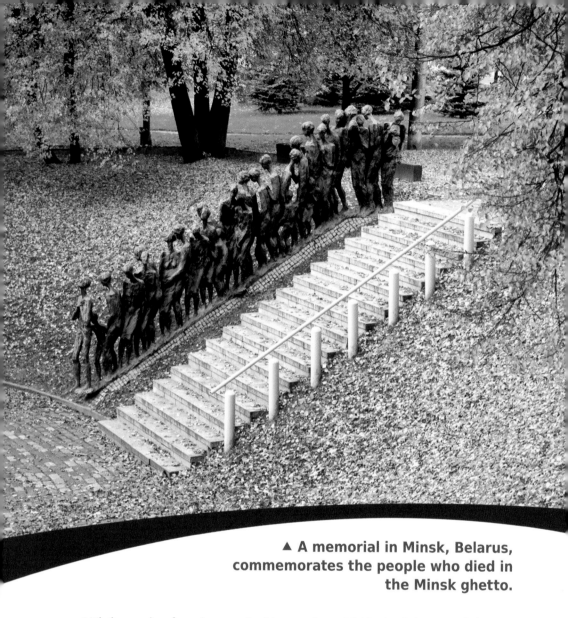

▲ **A memorial in Minsk, Belarus, commemorates the people who died in the Minsk ghetto.**

While at the farmhouse in November 1941, Jack learned the Nazis had shot his mother. Heartbroken, he decided to return to Mir and the ghetto. For months, Jack and a group of about 40 other people planned an escape. A German police officer, who was hiding his own Jewish identity, helped them.

He told the group that the ghetto would be emptied in mid-August 1942. He would lead the police out of Mir to look for Russian fighters. That would give Jack and his friends the opportunity to escape.

Jack and his friends escaped to the forest in small groups of five or six. Jack joined the resistance in the forest. He and his fellow escapees raided nearby farms for food. They stole weapons so they could hunt animals for food and defend themselves against Nazis. The Nazis had placed a price on their heads.

Rochelle came to the bunker in late 1942, as Jack had predicted. She had been forced to work at a sawmill in the Stolpce ghetto. But she managed to escape with three other women one foggy September morning. They swam across a river and hid in the forest. Rochelle had moved from one resistance group to another until a friend brought her to Jack's bunker.

Like Jack, Rochelle had lost family members. Nazis had taken her father from their house, and he never came back. She learned later that the Nazis had killed him. Her mother and sisters had been taken away, too.

Jack and Rochelle soon became friends, and the friendship turned into love. They married in an unofficial ceremony in the bunker on December 31, 1942.

As weeks passed and the weather grew colder, Jack did not know how they would survive the winter. Food would be scarce. He learned of a large resistance group of approximately 300 people in the forest. Jack and Rochelle met a member of this group. He invited them to join. Jack and Rochelle finally felt as if they had found a family.

In August 1943, Nazi soldiers, tanks, and airplanes raided the Naliboki Forest. Jack and Rochelle had to run. Although the Germans outnumbered them, the resistance group was more familiar with the forest. They knew the best places to hide. The Nazis' two-week raid was not successful.

In the spring of 1944, the resistance group learned that the Germans were in retreat. The Russian Army was only 30 miles (48 km) away. After a few days, the Russian Army freed the resistance fighters.

After the war, Jack and Rochelle immigrated to Saint Paul, Minnesota. Although they had an official marriage ceremony after the war, they celebrated their wedding anniversary as December 31, 1942.

◄ **The Nazis forced Jewish people into ghettos and, later, into concentration or death camps.**

Chapter 4

SIMON GRONOWSKI

On April 19, 1943, 11-year-old Simon Gronowski held tightly onto his mother in the cramped train car. They had been forced onto the train from a **detention camp** in Mechelen, Belgium. Simon did not know it at the time, but the train's destination was the Auschwitz death camp in Poland.

Simon and his mother stood in a back corner of the train car, gasping for air through a small vent in the roof. There was no food and nothing for them to drink, not even a sip of water.

Two months before, Simon and his family had been hiding in an apartment in Brussels, Belgium. Simon was sitting down to breakfast one morning with his mother and sister when two Gestapo agents barged in. Simon's father was in the hospital, so he was not with the family when the Nazis came. To protect his father, Simon's mother told the Nazis she was a widow.

The Gestapo agents took Simon, his mother, and his sister. They were brought to the Nazi headquarters in Brussels, Belgium.

◄ **Simon Gronowski escaped a transport that was headed to the Auschwitz death camp.**

▲ **In 2007, Simon visited the Jewish Museum of Deportation and Resistance in Mechelen, Belgium.**

These headquarters also served as a prison for Jewish people and a torture chamber for resistance fighters. The Nazis held the food or water for two nights. Then the detention camp in Mechelen. On April 16, 1943, they received the news that Simon and his mother would be put on a transport the following day.

The train left Mechelen at 10:00 p.m. on April 19. When it came to a bend, the train suddenly stopped. Simon heard shooting. One train car door, which had been bolted shut, opened. A Belgian resistance fighter yelled for them to get out. Some people jumped.

The train began to move again. Men throughout the train broke open doors with tools that had been left behind by the resistance fighters.

Simon's mother pressed a 100-franc note into his hand. He rolled it and hid it in his sock. She pushed him toward the door. Trees whooshed by, and wind whipped at his face. He stood at the edge.

THE JEWISH DEFENSE COMMITTEE

The train Simon had been on was the only train to Auschwitz that met with resistance. Simon owed his life to a Belgian resistance organization called the Jewish Defense Committee. Three Belgian men who were a part of the organization carried out the plan. They helped 233 of the 1,500 Jewish people on the train attempt escape. Of those who attempted to escape, 118 got away, including Simon. The Jewish Defense Committee also found hiding places in Belgium for approximately 14,000 Jewish people.

▲ Simon stands in front of a monument honoring the resistance fighters who helped save his life.

He was afraid to move. He was too small to reach the **foot rail**. His mother lifted him and set him down on the foot rail. The noise of the train deafened him. His mother released her grip. He jumped.

After Simon jumped, the train stopped. Nazis shot in his direction. He ran, although he wanted nothing more than to return to his mother. He tumbled down a hill and headed for the trees. All night, Simon traveled through fields and woods.

At daybreak, Simon spotted a farm. He knocked on the door. A woman answered. He stood before her in ripped clothes.

He told the woman he'd been playing with friends and gotten lost. She brought him to a local police officer. Any Belgian who did not turn a Jew into the police would be shot. Simon's heart raced as he stood before the policeman. He repeated his tale of playing with friends and getting lost.

Although the policeman figured Simon had come from the train, he and his wife fed and clothed him. They put Simon on a train back to Brussels. Simon reunited with his father. They hid with Catholic families for the rest of the war.

Simon never saw his mother and sister again. He later learned that the Nazis killed his mother on arrival at Auschwitz. His sister also died there.

THINK ABOUT IT

- What challenges did people fleeing the Nazis face?
- Why do you think some people hid during the Holocaust instead of attempting to escape?
- How might survivors who returned to their hometowns after the Holocaust have felt? How might their lives have been different after the war?

GLOSSARY

bunker (BUHNK-ur): A bunker is an underground hiding place. Jack and Rochelle hid from the Nazis in an underground bunker.

concentration camp (kon-sun-TRAY-shun KAMP): During World War II, a concentration camp was a place Hitler designed to imprison and starve Jewish people and other groups. Nina Klein's parents were sent to Theresienstadt, a concentration camp in German-occupied Czechoslovakia.

death camps (DETH KAMPS): Death camps were places Hitler designed to kill Jewish people and other prisoners through starvation or other means. Auschwitz and Treblinka were large death camps in Poland.

detention camp (di-TEN-shuhn KAMP): In Nazi Germany, a detention camp was a place where Jewish people and others were kept temporarily before being moved to concentration or death camps. The Gronowskis were kept in a detention camp in Mechelen, Belgium.

diplomat (DIP-luh-mat): A diplomat is someone who is given the responsibility to handle sensitive political matters. Sir Nicholas Winton was a British diplomat.

foot rail (FOOT RAYL): A foot rail is a rail used to help people step up into or step down from a train. Simon Gronowski escaped a train to Auschwitz by jumping off a foot rail.

interrogation (in-tayr-uh-GAY-shun): Interrogation is the act of asking a series of questions, usually to get someone to reveal key information. Irena Sendler was tortured at a Nazi interrogation center in Warsaw, Poland.

resistance (ri-ZISS-tuhnss): During World War II, the resistance was the unofficial armed forces that stood up against the Nazis. Jack Sutin and Rochelle Schleiff joined resistance groups.

TO LEARN MORE

Books

Rubin, Susan Goldman. *Irena Sendler and the Children of the Warsaw Ghetto*. New York, NY: Holiday House, 2011.

Strauss, Gwen. *The Hiding Game*. Gretna, LA: Pelican Publishing Company, 2017.

Zullo, Allan. *Escape: Children of the Holocaust*. New York, NY: Scholastic, 2009.

Web Sites

Visit our Web site for links about escaping Hitler:
childsworld.com/links

Note to Parents, Teachers, and Librarians: We routinely verify our Web links to make sure they are safe and active sites. So encourage your readers to check them out!

SELECTED BIBLIOGRAPHY

Bauer, Yehuda. *A History of the Holocaust*. Danbury, CT: Franklin Watts, 2001. Print.

Mazzeo, Tilar J. *Irena's Children: A True Story of Courage*. New York, NY: Gallery Books, 2016. Print.

Sutin, Jack, and Rochelle Sutin. *Jack & Rochelle: A Holocaust Story of Love and Resistance*. Minneapolis, MN: Graywolf Press, 1995. Print.

INDEX

ABOUT THE AUTHOR

Barbara Krasner is the author of more than 20 books for young readers. She specializes in twentieth-century American and Holocaust history. She teaches English and history at colleges and universities in New Jersey.